MINI-COCOTTE

TABLE OF CONTENTS
SAVORY COCOTTES

SWEET COCOTTES
TABLE OF CONTENTS

Stoneware
by **Le Creuset**

Since 1925, Le Creuset Cast Iron Cookware has been manufactured at a foundry in the town of Fresnoy le Grand approximately 120 miles north-east of Paris. Set among rolling hills and arable landscapes, the worlds largest, and oldest, manufacturer of high quality cast iron cookware distributes Le Creuset to every corner of the globe.

One of the first cooking utensils ever produced at the foundry was called a Cocotte. It is a cast iron French oven and this shape, and indeed the name, was the pivot of what is now an extensive range of cookware. Our Stoneware Mini Cocotte is a tribute to our cast iron heritage.

Le Creuset's Stoneware cooking and baking pieces are truly an All-in-One Dish - you can bake, slice, serve and store in it. Their classic design and bold, beautiful color adds a distinctive charm to any table.

Let Le Creuset bring any meal to the table in a gorgeous presentation. Le Creuset's stoneware range and the celebrated inimitable mini cocotte make any occasion feel special.

Le Creuset offers cookware in a wide range of colors.
Bright vibrant colors, pastels and neutrals, from the most classical to the most contemporary, enabling you to match your cookware to your home décor and tableware.

Resistant

Safe

Practical

Durability

- Le Creuset's virtually non-porous Stoneware is fired at 2156°F, giving it unmatched strength and durability - and making it resistant to chipping, cracking, and staining.

- Suitable for use in the oven up to 260°C / 500°F & under the Grill / Broiler.

+260°C ▮ +500°F
-18°C ▯ 0°F

Ease of Handling

- Our Stoneware features sure-grip knobs, handles, and rims, to allow for easy handling and confident use.

- Totally hygienic cooking surface, Le Creuset Stoneware will not absorb odors or flavors, and it resists moisture absorption.

Enameled Surface

- Its enameled surface makes each piece easy to clean and scratch resistant so that it looks and performs wonderfully for years to come.

- Adapted to everyday cooking.

- Soft and homogeneous baking.

- Keeps ingredients cool as well as hot.

- Microwave, Freezer and Dishwasher safe.

Oven	Grill / Broiler	Microwave	Freezer	Dishwasher	DO NOT use any piece on direct heat source.

LE CREUSET

LE CREUSET
stoneware range

Square Dish

Rectangular Dishes

Oval Dishes

Deep Dish Casseroles

Square Casserole
with Lid

Rectangular Casserole with
Lid

Oval Casserole
with Lid

Round Casserole
with Lid

Petite Tart Dish

Tart Dish

Pie Dish

Loaf Pan

French Onion Soup
Bowl

Mini Round
Cocotte

Mini Oval
Cocotte

Petite Au Gratin
Dish

Wok Dish

Oval Bowl

Ramekin

Utensil Crocks

Pitcher

Small Teapot w/infuser

Citrus Juicer

Salt/Pepper Shakers

Mortar and Pestle

Spoon Rest

Batter Bowl

Mixing Bowls

Canisters

Butter Dish

Spice Jars

Mini cocottes are available in 8 colors:

White

Cobalt

Dijon

Black Onyx

Flame

Cherry

Caribbean

Kiwi

Our stoneware range varies country to country.
Please visit our website at **Lecreuset.com** to see our latest range of products

SAVORY COCOTTES

CHICKEN POT
PIES

MINI LEEK GRATINS
WITH CREAM AND MUSTARD

MINI CHERRY TOMATO
TATINS

WILD MUSHROOM
RISOTTO

MINI ONION
SOUPS

MINI SPINACH
SOUFFLÉS

SWEET POTATO
PECAN CRUMBLES

ARTICHOKES
"À LA PROVENÇALE"

CHICKEN TAGINES
WITH APRICOTS, FIGS AND ALMONDS

SCRAMBLED EGGS
WITH HERBS, SALMON AND CREAM CHEESE

LITTLE SWISS
COCOTTES

LITTLE THAI
COCOTTES

RAVIOLI GRATINS
WITH GOAT CHEESE, BASIL PISTOU AND PINE NUTS

MACARONI AND FOUR CHEESE
GRATINS

SHIRRED EGGS
WITH SMOKED HAM AND GINGERBREAD SOLDIERS

CHICKEN POT PIES

- **4** chicken breasts
- **7 oz (1 ¼ sticks)** sweet butter
- **4** carrots
- **3/4 cup** pearl onions
- **4 cups** chicken stock
- **2 tbsps** unbleached flour
- **3/4 cup** half and half

- **3/4 cup** of peas
- **1 tsp** parsley chopped fine
- **1** frozen pre-rolled puff pastry dough
- **2** egg yolks beaten with 1 tsp of milk
- **S**alt and freshly ground pepper

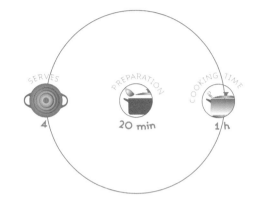

SERVES 4 · PREPARATION 20 min · COOKING TIME 1/h

Preheat the oven to 350°F.

Put the chicken breasts on a baking sheet covered with parchment paper and baste with 1 oz of softened butter. Salt and pepper generously. Bake for 20 minutes. When the chicken is cooked through, cut it into large chunks.

Peel the carrots and cut them into small dice. Peel the pearl onions. In a small sauce pan, bring the chicken stock to a boil then set aside.

In a large casserole: melt the remaining 6 oz of butter. Cook the pearl onions for 10 to 15 minutes slowly over a low flame, until they are translucent and caramelized. Add the flour and continue cooking for 2 minutes stirring continuously. Add the hot chicken stock. Let it simmer for 1 minute till the sauce begins to thicken and loses the taste of flour. Add the half and half, 1 teaspoon of salt, a half teaspoon of ground pepper, the chunks of chicken, the diced carrots, the peas, and the parsley. Give it a good stir.

Increase the oven temperature to 400°F.

Divide the preparation into 4 mini cocottes. Cut 4 circles of puff pastry dough slightly larger than the mini cocottes. Moisten the edges of the cocottes with the egg wash. Place one circle on each filled cocotte, pressing down around to seal the dough circle. Cut a small hole in the center to make a steam vent.

With a pastry brush, coat the dough tops with egg wash. Bake for 15—20 minutes or until golden brown.

Replace the green peas with 7 oz of fresh asparagus tips cut into 1 inch chunks, and you have a gourmet variation on this classic dish!

MINI LEEK GRATINS WITH CREAM AND MUSTARD

SERVES
4

PREPARATION
15 min

COOKING TIME
30 min

- 4 1½ inches in diameter leeks
- **3/4 cup** chicken stock
- **3/4 cup** heavy cream
- **1 tbsp** grainy mustard
- Salt and peper

Preheat the oven to 350°F.

Wash the leeks. Use only the white part (keep the green part for a vegetable soup). Cut the white stalks in half and carefully rinse with cold running water, removing all trace of sand or earth. Cut each stalk into pieces 2 inches long.

Bring the chicken stock to a boil then let it cool. Whisk in the cream and mustard.

Par-boil the leeks for 3 minutes in salted water. Stop the cooking by rinsing them under cold water.

Divide the leeks between 4 mini cocottes. Pour several spoonfuls of the mustard cream mixture over top each one. Bake for 20 minutes. Serve hot and bubbly!

Turnip fans! Replace the leeks with the same quantity of peeled turnips. Cut them into chunks. Plunge these for 10 min in boiling water. Then sauté them for 10 min with a spot of olive oil. And continue as with leeks.

MINI CHERRY TOMATO
TATINS

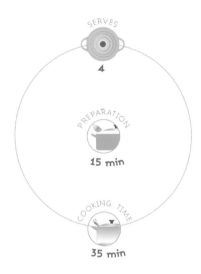

SERVES

4

PREPARATION

15 min

COOKING TIME

35 min

- 1 ¼ lb of ripe cherry tomatoes
- 2 tbsps of olive oil
- 2 garlic cloves, minced
- 1 tbsp of sugar
- 1 frozen pre-rolled pie crust
- "Fleur de sel" and freshly ground pepper

Preheat the oven to 325°F.

Thaw frozen pie crust.

Rinse the cherry tomatoes and pat dry.

Heat the oil in a large heavy frying pan. Add the minced garlic, the cherry tomatoes and the sugar. Cook over a low flame for 5 minutes (not longer or the tomatoes will burst). Divide both the tomatoes and their juices between 4 mini cocottes.

Cut 4 circles of pie crust slightly larger in diameter than a mini cocotte. Place 1 circle over each cocotte, folding the excess into the interior.

Bake for 30 minutes on a baking sheet covered with aluminium foil.

On removal from the oven, let cool for 10 minutes and overturn each tatin onto a small plate.

Salt and pepper and serve immediately.

These also work as a "sweet" version! Remember that the tomato is a fruit! To make this delicious dessert, replace the garlic with 2 tbsps of candied ginger chopped into tiny cubes!

WILD MUSHROOM
RISOTTO

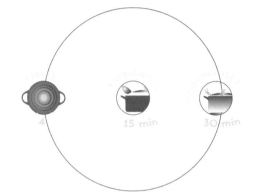

- **1 lb** wild mushrooms (or a combination of fresh shitake and portobello)
- **8 cups** chicken stock
- **1 tbsp** olive oil
- **1** onion minced fine
- **2** cloves minced garlic
- **2 ½ cups** Arborio or Carnaroli risotto rice

- **3/4 cup** dry white wine
- **2 tbsps** chopped lemon thyme
- **3 tbsps** chopped parsley
- **1 tbsp** melted butter
- **4 oz** Parmigiano Reggiano
- **T**ruffle oil and chopped parsley for the decoration

Carefully wash the mushrooms, cap and all. Separate the caps from the stems. Slice the caps into large chunks of more or less the same size. Mince the stems. Peel and mince the onion and garlic.

Heat the chicken stock over a low flame.

Heat 1 tablespoon of olive oil. Add half of the minced onion and garlic. Slowly cook until translucent. Almost 5 minutes. Add the mushrooms, herbs and butter. Sauté the mushrooms for 3-5 minutes until they lose their juices and brown slightly. Add salt and pepper and let them continue to cook for another minute and remove from heat.

Heat 2 tablespoons of olive oil in a large pan. Add the other half of the onion and garlic. Add the rice and continue stirring for one minute until the rice becomes translucent. Add the wine and reduce it almost entirely. Add one ladle full of the hot stock. Continue to cook, uncovered, never ceasing to stir, until the rice has fully absorbed the liquid. Little by little add the rest of the stock, leaving the time for the rice to absorb the stock. Pay strict attention to the time. In twenty minutes the rice should be both « al dente » and creamy.

At the end of cooking, add the grated parmesan and the sautéed mushrooms. And don't skimp on the parmigiano reggiano! Get the real thing and grate it yourself!

Continue cooking for a brief moment to melt the cheese.

Last Touch? Add a several drops of truffle oil and finely chopped parsley.

Pass 4 mini cocottes under hot water and quickly dry them. A portion of hot risotto in each, and serve immediately!

The wild mushroom season is short! For the rest of the year use flavorful dried mushrooms: ceps or « boletus edulis », morels and chanterelles soaked in a cupful of hot water for 15 min. Don't throw out the water, strain it and add it to the stock for the risotto!

MINI ONION SOUPS

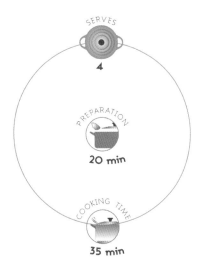

SERVES
4

PREPARATION
20 min

COOKING TIME
35 min

- 5 **large yellow onions**
- 3 oz (3/4 stick) **butter**
- 4 cups **beef stock**
- 1 **laurel leaf and 3 branches of lemon thyme**
- 4 **thick slices of crusty bread**
- 2 **small onions**
- 4 oz **gruyere, grated**

Preheat the oven to 400°F.

Peel and chop the larger onions. Heat 2 oz of butter in a heavy bottomed frying pan. Cook the onions over a low flame for 20 minutes, until they are translucent and caramelized. It is this slow caramelization that gives the soup its entire flavor. So don't rush it! Add the beef stock, the laurel leaf and the lemon thyme and let this simmer for 10 minutes. Divide the hot broth between 4 mini cocottes.

Cut the 4 slices of crusty bread into 4 "tops" slightly larger than the diameter of a cocotte. Peel and cut the 2 smaller onions in half. Make a small hole in the center of the slices of bread and push half an onion into each.

Carefully pan fry in the remaining butter, each slice, onion side down till the onion is golden and caramelized.

Place each "top" on its mini cocotte and sprinkle with grated cheese.

Bake 5 min or until the cheese has melted and become a crusty golden brown. Serve immediately.

These can be prepared up to 48 hours in advance. In this case, prepare the broth ahead of time. Make the "tops" and warm up in the oven before serving. Indeed, the soup will have an even deeper, richer flavor.

MINI SPINACH SOUFFLES

- **5 oz** baby spinach leaves
- **1 ½ oz (1/3 stick)** butter
- **1/2 cup** flour
- **2 egg yolks**
- **2 cups** warm milk

- **4 oz** freshly grated Parmigiano Reggiano
- **5 egg whites**
- **Salt** and freshly ground pepper

SERVES 4

PREPARATION 20 min

COOKING TIME 25 to 35 min

Preheat the oven to 400°F.

Butter 4 mini cocottes.

Wash and dry the baby spinach carefully. Mix in a blender and set aside.

Prepare the béchamel:

Melt the butter in a small pan. Add the flour and cook for 3 minutes, stirring with a wooden spoon, until the flour taste has disappeared. Set aside.

In a mixing bowl, whisk the egg yolks. Add the mixture of butter and flour. Add little by little, the warmed milk, whisking as you go. Add the blended spinach and half of the grated parmesan. Salt and pepper to taste. Set aside and let the mixture cool.

In a large mixing bowl, whisk the egg whites with a pinch of salt, until they form rigid peaks. Fold in carefully and with a light hand, 1/3 of the spinach béchamel. Fold in the rest of the spinach so that the color is well distributed. Don't over stir!

Fill each mini cocotte 3/4 full. Sprinkle the rest of the grated parmesan on top. Run your little finger around the rim of each soufflé. This will "encourage" the soufflés to rise and expand vertically from the top of the cocotte.

Place them carefully on a baking sheet. Bake for 20-30 minutes or until the tops are golden brown.

Careful ! With a convection oven, the top will color a bit quicker than the interior. Halfway through the cooking, cover the soufflés with a large piece of aluminium foil. Serve immediately.

A mini soufflé is easier to make than a large one and it has more of those delicious crusty bits! Fresh Baby spinach leaves are the perfect ingredient for this recipe. They contain less water than larger spinach leaves, and don't need to be parboiled. They'll keep that beautiful bright green color !

SWEET POTATO PECAN CRUMBLES

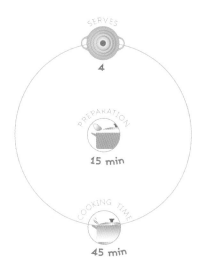

SERVES
4

PREPARATION
15 min

COOKING TIME
45 min

- 2 ¼ lbs sweet potatoes
- 1/4 cup flour
- 1/4 cup dark brown sugar
- 1/2 tsp pumpkin pie spices
- 2 oz (1/2 stick) sweet butter, well chilled and cut into small cubes
- 2 oz pecans
- 1/4 cup maple syrup

Preheat the oven to 350°F.

Lightly butter 4 mini cocottes.

In a medium sized mixing bowl, add the sugar and spices to the flour. With your finger tips, swiftly work the cold butter into the dry ingredients. It should look like corn meal. Careful! Proceed quickly. If your ingredients become too warm, put the bowl immediately into the refrigerator for 15 minutes until all is very well chilled and begin again.

Peel the sweet potatoes and cut them diagonally into ¼ inch slices. Divide these between the 4 mini cocottes. Sprinkle each with half of the "crumble" mixture. Layer the rest of the sweet potatoes slices with the remaining "crumble". Scatter the pecans and moisten each with the maple syrup.

Cover with a sheet of aluminium foil and bake alongside your roast for 45 minutes. Remove the foil after 30 minutes. Serve piping hot!

This Thanksgiving favorite is an excellent accompaniment to roast chicken or pork loin.

ARTICHOKES
"À LA PROVENÇALE"

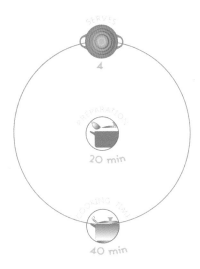

SERVES
4

PREPARATION
20 min

COOKING TIME
40 min

- **20** baby artichokes or 4 large ones
- **2** shallots
- **5** garlic cloves
- **6 tbsps** olive oil
- **Z**est and juice of one lemon
- **1 ¼ cup** of dry white wine
- **2 tbsps** thyme or lemon thyme
- **S**alt and pepper

Preheat oven to 350°F.

Cut the stems off of the baby artichokes leaving a scant inch. Peel the remaining stems, removing the fibrous threads. Remove the tough outer leaves and cut the artichokes by 3/4, removing the tops of the leaves as well. Cut in half and remove the choke. Cut into 4 pieces if you are using larger artichokes.

Peel and mince the shallots and garlic. In a small pan, gently cook both over a low flame, in the olive oil until they are translucent and caramelized. Add the artichokes, the lemon juice and cook uncovered for 10 minutes.

Add the white wine, the lemon zest and the thyme. Reduce the liquids another 10 minutes to a syrupy consistency.

Divide between 4 mini cocottes and bake with the lid on, for 20 minutes.

Salt and pepper to taste and serve immediately.

These are the perfect vegetable to accompany a baked sea bass! Bake them right alongside the fish for 20 minutes.

CHICKEN TAGINES
WITH APRICOTS, FIGS AND ALMONDS

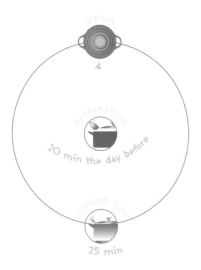

SERVES
4

PREPARATION
20 min the day before

COOKING TIME
25 min

- **1 ¾ lb** boneless, skinless chicken breast cut into bite size pieces
- **6 tbsps** olive oil
- Juice of 2 lemons
- **1 tbsp** chopped fresh coriander
- **1 tbsp** chopped fresh parsley
- **1 tbsp** chopped fresh mint leaves
- **1 tbsp** grated ginger root
- **1** pinch saffron filaments
- **1** onion
- **1** clove garlic
- **2 tbsps** honey
- **4** dried apricots
- **4** dried figs
- **2 tbsps** golden raisins or dried currants
- **2 tbsps** peeled almonds
- **1/2 cup** water

The night before, in a large bowl, coat the chicken pieces with a marinade of 4 tablespoons olive oil, the juice of one lemon, the grated ginger, the minced onion and garlic, as well as the chopped coriander, parsley and mint. Add the filaments of saffron. Toss until well coated. Cover and place in an airtight container, in the refrigerator until the following day.

The next day:

Preheat the oven to 400°F.

Strain the chicken and set aside the remaining marinade.

Heat 2 tablespoons of olive oil in a large frying pan. Brown the chicken carefully on all sides over a low flame. Add the reserved marinade, honey, the apricots, figs, raisins, almonds and 1/2 cup of water. Let it simmer covered for 5 minutes.

Divide the cooked chicken among the cocottes. Bake, covered for an additional 10 minutes.

Serve immediately.

Accompany these with a plain couscous, served too in a mini cocotte!

SCRAMBLED EGGS
WITH HERBS, SALMON AND CREAM CHEESE

SERVES
4

PREPARATION
10 min

COOKING TIME
20 min

- 8 large eggs
- 8 slices of challah bread or brioche
- 1 minced onion
- 4 pieces of thinly sliced smoked salmon, cut into long ribbons
- 3 tbsps of milk
- 4 tbsps of mixed chopped chives, tarragon, chervil, and parsley
- 2 oz (1/2 stick) butter
- 4 oz cream cheese
- Salt and freshly ground pepper

Preheat 4 mini-cocottes in a 300°F oven for 15 minutes.

Toast 8 slices of challah. Cut 8 circles of the diameter of a cocotte from the heart of each slice.

Put a toasted circle in each cocotte. Reserve the other four circles for the tops!

In a mixing bowl, whisk the eggs with the milk and 2 tablespoons of the chopped herbs.

Melt the butter in a medium sized frying pan over a low flame. Add the minced onion and cook until transparent and caramelized, almost 15 minutes. Add the eggs and the cream cheese. Let cook 4 minutes, stirring from time to time. Add the ribbons of smoked salmon and cook without stirring for 1 more minute. The eggs should be cooked but still have a moist look. Salt and freshly ground pepper to taste.

Divide the scrambled eggs between the four mini cocottes. Scatter the remaining chopped herbs and top with the last 4 circles of toasted challah. Serve immediately.

For a special occasion, add 1 tbsp of vodka to the onions during cooking and 1 tbsp of salmon caviar on top of each mini cocotte!

LITTLE SWISS COCOTTES

SERVES
4

PREPARATION
20 min

COOKING TIME
15 min

Fondue:
- **1/2 lb** Fontina
- **1/2 lb** Swiss Gruyere
- **2** cloves of garlic
- **1 tsp** corn starch
- **1** pinch of baking soda
- **1 cup** of dry white wine
- **F**reshly ground pepper

Vegetables:
- **B**roccoli
- **C**auliflower
- **C**arrot sticks
- **F**ennel
- **J**uice of 1 lemon

Equipment:
- **F**ondue forks or bamboo skewers

Preheat the oven to 350°F.

Peel the cloves of garlic and rub them on the insides of 4 mini cocottes.

Place the mini cocottes on a baking sheet and pop them into the oven.

During this time, cut off the rind of both cheeses and cut both cheeses into tiny cubes.

Sprinkle the corn starch over the cheese. Mix the baking soda with one teaspoon of hot water in a small glass. Reserve.

Parboil the vegetables in small quantities 1 minute in salted boiling water. Douse the fennel with a bit of lemon juice immediately after cooking to keep it from discoloring. Keep the vegetables in a warm place while you prepare the fondue.

In a heavy bottom pan, melt the cheese with the white wine, stirring without stopping with a wooden spoon. At the last minute, when everything has melted, add the baking soda. Give it a good stir quickly as the baking soda will make the fondue foam up. Take the pan off the heat.

Divide the fondue into the oven-hot mini cocottes. Add one pinch of freshly ground pepper and serve immediately with the warm vegetables.

One dish: two cheeses.
One creamy, one full of flavor.
Cheese doesn't like a high heat so don't be tempted to up the flame to cut down on cooking time. The Swiss don't drink cold liquids with their fondues. They swear by hot tea!

LITTLE THAI COCOTTES

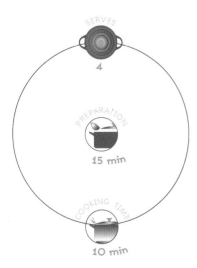

SERVES
4

PREPARATION
15 min

COOKING TIME
10 min

- **24** peeled raw shrimp
- **12** ears of baby corn
- **6** white button mushrooms
- **4** cloves of garlic
- **1** small can of coconut milk
- **2 cups** of chicken stock
- **2 stalks** of fresh lemongrass
  (10 if you are using 8 as skewers)

- **4** kaffir lime leaves (asian grocery in frozen section)
- **J**uice of 1 lime
- **2 tbsps** of freshly grated ginger root
- **1** tiny red thai chili, seeds removed
- **F**resh coriander leaves

Carefully thread 3 shrimp onto 8, –4 inches– bamboo skewers (Cut them if they are too long!).

Cut the baby corn in half length-wise. Cut the mushrooms into thin slices. Peel and mince the garlic cloves.

Place all of the ingredients in a large pan (except the skewered shrimp and the coriander leaves).

Bring to boiling point and simmer for 10 minutes. Add the skewered shrimp at the last minute of cooking.

Divide the soup between 4 mini cocottes. Place 2 shrimp skewers in each. Add several fresh coriander leaves and serve piping hot!

Don't panic! You will find all of these ingredients in your local asian or vietnamese grocery! Use the thin hard hearts of 8 long stalks of lemongrass as skewers. It adds a hint more flavor!

RAVIOLI GRATINS
WITH GOAT CHEESE, BASIL PISTOU AND 'PINE NUTS'

SERVES
4

PREPARATION
20 min

COOKING TIME
10 min

- 4 oz crumbly fresh goat cheese
- 2 bunches of fresh basil
- 4 cloves of garlic
- Several drops of olive oil
- 2 tbsps (1/4 stick) sweet butter
- 3/4 cup cream
- One 8 oz package of quality frozen cheese ravioli

- 2 oz pine nuts
- 4 tbsps of freshly grated Parmigiano Reggiano
- Pine nuts and fresh basil leaves for decoration

Prepare the basil pistou: Rinse the basil leaves under cold water. Gently dry with in a clean kitchen towel. Peel the garlic and take out the inner germ. With a small mixer, mix the garlic with the basil and a few drops of olive oil.

Precook the ravioli for one minute in salted boiling water, taking care to drain them well. Add several drops of olive oil to coat them and prevent them from sticking together.

Preheat the oven to 400°F.

Lightly butter 4 mini cocottes.

Add to each, a layer of ravioli, a spoonful of crumbled goat cheese and one of the basil pistou. Add one teaspoon of pine nuts and continue with another layer of ravioli, one tablespoon of cream, one of goat cheese and a last one of pistou. End with a layer of ravioli, a tablespoon of cream and a generous amount of grated parmesan.

Bake, uncovered for about 10 minutes until the tops look crunchy and a deep golden brown.

Just before serving, add several fresh, roughly chopped basil leaves and a teaspoon of pine nuts scattered on top.

For the mini gourmet touch : add thin strips of roasted red pepper along with 1 tbsp of their cooking juices to each mini cocotte.

MACARONI AND FOUR CHEESE GRATINS

SERVES
4

PREPARATION
20 min

COOKING TIME
15 min

- **18 oz** winter durum wheat macaroni
- **1 oz (1/4 stick)** sweet butter
- **1/2 cup** heavy cream
- **2 oz** Gorgonzola
- **2 oz** Fontina
- **2 oz** Marscarpone
- **2 oz** Parmigiano Reggiano
- **2 oz** chopped walnuts
- **S**alt and freshly ground pepper

Preheat the oven to 430°F. Lightly butter 4 mini cocottes.

Plunge the macaroni a good minute in boiling salted water. They should not be cooked through. Pass the pasta under cold running water to stop them cooking. Add several drops of canola or simple vegetable oil to keep it from sticking together.

Melt the butter in a small pan over a low flame. Add the cream, the Gorgonzola, the Fontina, the Marscarpone and the Parmigiano Reggiano (reserving 4 tablespoons for the top). Stir the cheese until all are well melted. Add salt and freshly ground pepper to taste. Add the chopped walnuts.

Add the cooked pasta to the sauce and divide into 4 mini-cocottes. Sprinkle the rest of the Parmigiano Reggiano over each cocotte. Bake for 10 to 15 minutes or until the tops are golden brown and crusty looking. On taking them out of the oven, let them rest for 5 minutes before serving.

Cheeses with higher fat content melt better than those that with a lower one! So combine your favorites: creamy Fontina, Gorgonzola, buffalo mozzarella, Parmigano Reggiano.

A mini cocotte offers the perfect portion of this rich but oh so delicious favorite!

SHIRRED EGGS
WITH SMOKED HAM
AND GINGERBREAD SOLDIERS

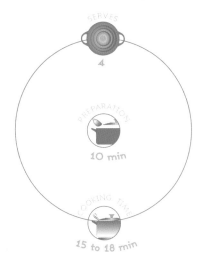

SERVES
4

PREPARATION
10 min

COOKING TIME
15 to 18 min

- **8** extra large, extra fresh eggs
- **4** slices of challah or brioche
- **4** slices of dense gingerbread or pain d'épices
- **4 tbsps** sour cream
- **1 oz** smoked ham cut into small cubes
- "**F**leur de sel" and freshly ground pepper

Preheat the oven to 350°F.

Lightly butter 4 mini cocottes.

Cut 4 circles of brioche lightly smaller than the diameter of a mini cocotte (about 3 inches). Cut little thin sticks of gingerbread : 3 inches by ½ inch and lightly toast them in the oven on a baking sheet with the circles of brioche. Both burn easily so keep your eye on them!

Place one toasted circle of brioche in each cocotte.

Break two eggs on top of each brioche. Put 1 tablespoon of sour cream in each cocotte.

Place the four filled cocottes into a shallow baking pan. Pour boiling water in the pan to make a "bain-marie". Bake, uncovered, for 15 minutes (18 minutes if you prefer your eggs well-cooked) or until the white is firm.

Cut the smoked ham into small cubes and scatter on the baked eggs with a pinch of "fleur de sel" and one of freshly ground pepper. Serve immediately with the toasted gingerbread sticks.

To really capture the full flavor of this dish, use only the freshest eggs, the best ham, fleur de sel and freshly ground pepper!

SWEET COCOTTES

CINNAMON APPLES

CHOCOLATE COCOTTES WITH MOLTEN HEARTS

CHERRY RASPBERRY CLAFOUTIS

PEAR BREAD PUDDINGS

PEACH CRUMBLES

DELICATE ALMOND MILK PUDDINGS

LITTLE COCONUT FLANS

LEMON MERINGUE CUSTARDS

UPSIDE DOWN PLUM TARTS

FROZEN SOUFFLÉS OF ROSE AND VIOLETTE

CINNAMON APPLES

SERVES
4

PREPARATION
15 min

COOKING TIME
40 min

- 4 Golden Delicious apples
- 1/4 cup light brown sugar
- 1/2 tsp of ground cinnamon
- 1/2 tsp of ground nutmeg
- 4 tbsps (1/2 stick) sweet butter cut into little cubes
- 3/4 cup maple syrup

Preheat oven to 350°F. Lightly butter 4 mini cocottes.

Wash the apples. Cut the tops off of each apple. With an apple corer, take out the woody center and set an apple in each cocotte on a baking sheet covered with aluminium foil.

Mix the brown sugar with the cinnamon and the nutmeg. Fill each apple with one tablespoon of the cinnamon sugar. Reserve the rest. Sprinkle 2 tablespoons of the butter cubes over the apples, put their tops back on and pop them in the oven for 35 minutes, uncovered.

While the apples are in the oven, melt the remaining 2 tablespoons of butter in a small pan and add the remaining cinnamon, nutmeg and sugar as well as the maple syrup. Reduce this by half.

When the apples are finished baking, add a spoonful of the reduced syrup and serve immediately.

In other seasons, try other fruits!

Peaches, ripe and juicy, are wonderful! Leaving them whole, peel the peaches by plunging into boiling water for 2 min. No need to take the pit out. Melt 1/4 cup of apricot preserves. Proceed as with the apples, baking the peaches for 35 min. Baste each peach several times with the melted preserves.

CHOCOLATE COCOTTES WITH MOLTEN HEARTS

- **7 oz bittersweet chocolate**
- **6 oz (1 ½ sticks) butter**
- **4 large egg yolks**
- **4 large whole eggs**

- **1/2 cup** sugar
- **2/3 cup** unbleached flour
- **Zest of 1 orange**

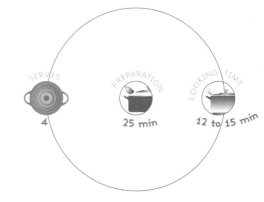

SERVES 4 · PREPARATION 25 min · COOKING TIME 12 to 15 min

Preheat oven to 400°F.

Butter and flour 4 mini cocottes, tapping out any excess flour.

In the top of a double boiler, melt the chocolate and butter together. Stir until well blended, then let cool to warm room temperature.

In a large bowl, whisk the egg yolks and whole eggs together, then beat in the sugar a tablespoon at a time. Continue beating until the eggs have tripled in volume, and are a pale yellow color. This may take upwards of 15 minutes, 4 minutes with an electric whisk!

Fold the beaten eggs into the chocolate and gently blend the two.

Sprinkle the flour into the cooled chocolate mixture, little by little and continue mixing until well blended.

Add the orange zest. Save a few strands for decoration.

Divide the batter into the four prepared cocottes and place, uncovered, in the oven on a baking sheet.

Bake for 12-15 minutes. When done, the batter will have puffed up. When you move the baking sheet slightly, it won't jiggle in the center.

Dust the tops with powdered cocoa and garnish with reserved orange zest. Serve immediatly.

Use only the best quality chocolate available. Callebaut or Valrhona Noir Gastronomie with 65% cocoa works brilliantly!

SWEET COCOTTES
p.44

CHERRY RASPBERRY
CLAFOUTIS

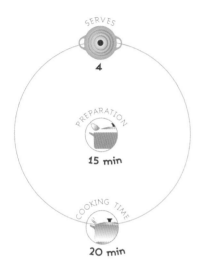

SERVES
4

PREPARATION
15 min

COOKING TIME
20 min

- 2 cups pitted cherries
- 1¼ cup raspberries
- 1 cup flour
- 3 egg yolks
- 3/4 cup powdered sugar

- 1 tsp baking powder
- 1 pinch of salt
- 1 cup heavy cream
- Powdered sugar for decoration

Preheat oven to 400°F.

Lightly butter 4 mini cocottes.

Clafoutis batter: combine flour, powdered sugar, baking powder and salt. Add the cream and mix well.

Divide the fruits between the 4 mini cocottes and place on a baking sheet. Add a small ladleful of the batter to each. Bake for 5 minutes. Add the rest of the batter to each cocotte and continue baking for another 15 minutes until the tops are a deep golden brown.

Let cool to room temperature. Dust with powdered sugar before serving.

Cinnamon lovers, discover the subtle association between cinnamon and all red berries!

Add a pinch of cinnamon to the clafoutis batter and voilà!

PEAR BREAD PUDDINGS

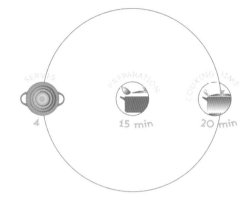

- **4** ripe pears (thin skinned comice are best)
- **Z**est and juice of one lemon
- **12** half inch slices of challah bread (or brioche)

- **2 cups** milk
- **1/4 cup** sugar
- **1** vanilla bean
- **4** eggs
- **P**owdered sugar for decoration

SERVES 4

PREPARATION 15 min

COOKING TIME 20 min

Preheat the oven to 375°F.

Lightly butter 4 mini cocottes.

Wash and dry the pears. Peel 3 of them, reserving the fourth. Cut the peeled pears in two and remove the woody center. Slice the halves into long thin pieces. Sprinkle lemon juice over the slices to keep them from discoloring.

Cut 12 circles of challah, the same diameter as the mini-cocotte. No cookie cutter that size? Try scissors!

In a small pan, heat the milk. Add the sugar and vanilla bean, split in half, stirring till the sugar has completely dissolved. Take it off the flame and let it rest for 10 minutes. Remove the vanilla bean.

In a mixing bowl, beat the eggs. Pour in the cooled milk, little by little. Add the lemon zest.

Put one circle of challah in the bottom of each cocotte. Cover with a large spoonful of the batter. Place a layer of sliced pears. Continue layering: challah, batter, pear, ending with challah bread till you have reached the top.

Why not try the unusual but delicious addition of star anise to this dessert? 3 pods broken off of one star anise is quite enough to perfume the heating milk mixture. Take the pods out before mixing the milk with the eggs.

Cut the last unpeeled pear in long thin slices and place these carefully on the top circle of challah. A last spoonful of the batter, and they are ready for the oven.

Bake for 15 – 20 minutes, uncovered.

Dust powdered sugar over each cocotte and serve immediately.

PEACH
CRUMBLES

SERVES

4

PREPARATION

15 min

COOKING TIME

25 min

- **6** ripe peaches (about 2 lbs)
- **1 cup** sugar
- **Zest** and juice of 1 lemon
- **1/4 tsp** of ground cinnamon

- **1 cup** unbleached flour
- **4 oz (1 stick)** butter (very cold and cut into little cubes)
- **1/3 cup** walnuts

Preheat oven to 375°F.

Lightly butter 4 mini cocottes.

Prepare the peaches. To remove the skin, plunge the peaches into a pan of boiling water, one by one, for 2 minutes.

Take them out with a slotted spoon, peel them, sprinkle a few drops of lemon juice over each one and let cool. Cut into generous chunks. Mix with 1/2 cup of the sugar, the lemon zest, and the cinnamon.

Mix the remaining sugar, 1/2 cup, with the flour and the little cubes of chilled butter. With your finger tips, quickly mix the 3 ingredients together. It should look like rough cornmeal. If your mixture is too warm, put the bowl into the refrigerator for 15 minutes. Start again when all is well chilled.

Chop the nuts and add them to the topping mixture. Fill 4 mini cocottes with the fruit and add the topping to each.

Place the mini cocottes on a baking sheet covered with aluminium foil as peaches are very juicy!

Bake for 20 minutes, uncovered.

Serve these hot out of the oven or room temperature.

Use any stone fruit for these fruit crumbles. Peaches, apricots, plums, anything ripe, available locally and in season! Save any extra crumble made by freezing it in small ziploc bags.

DELICATE ALMOND MILK PUDDINGS

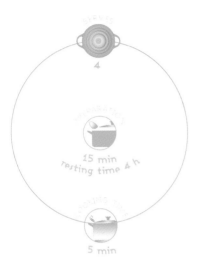

- **4 cups** almond milk
- **1 pkg** gelatin (or 1 tsp agar-agar)
- **3/4 cup** half and half
- **1/4 cup** sugar
- **1 tbsp** orange flower water
- **A** pinch of salt
- **Z**est of 1 lemon

- **B**lanched whole almonds and ground cinnamon for decoration

Soften gelatin in 1/3 cup of the almond milk. Heat till boiling, stirring constantly, till the gelatin (or agar agar) has completely dissolved (5 minutes). Add the rest of the almond milk and bring it again to a boil. Take it off the heat and add the orange flower water and the salt.

Let cool to room temperature. Fill 4 mini cocottes. Cover and let "set" in the refrigerator for at least four hours.

Before serving, add a blanched almond, a bit of lemon zest and a pinch of cinnamon.

If you use agar-agar for this recipe, 1 tsp should do it. It is a good choice for the summer months, as it sets at room temperature. Orange flower water is available in middle-eastern groceries or specialty shops.

LITTLE COCONUT FLANS

SERVES
4

PREPARATION
10 min

COOKING TIME
1 h 10

- **1 ½ cup** freshly grated coconut
- **4 cups** skimmed milk
- **1** vanilla bean
- **8** large eggs
- **1/3 cup** sugar

- **3/4 cup** coconut cream
- **1/2 cup** coconut ribbons for decoration

Preheat the oven to 375°F.

Spread the coconut ribbons on a baking sheet covered with parchment paper. Bake for about 10 minutes or until golden brown.

Split a vanilla bean in two and scrape the seeds. In a medium sized pan, bring to boiling point the skimmed milk and the vanilla seeds. Remove from heat and set aside to cool.

In a large mixing bowl, whisk together the egg yolks with the sugar until the mixture is a pale yellow color (about 4 minutes). Add the cooled milk little by little to the eggs and sugar.

Add the grated coconut and the coconut cream.

Divide the preparation between four mini cocottes. Pour a good inch of boiling water in a deep sided baking pan to make a bain marie. Put the cocottes in the pan and bake uncovered for 50 minutes. Sprinkle with the toasted coconut ribbons and serve slightly cooled but still warm.

While toasting ribbon coconut in the oven: don't take your eyes off of it! Coconut goes from "toasted" to "burnt" in seconds!

LEMON MERINGUE
CUSTARDS

Custard:
- 3 large eggs separated
- 2 cups whole milk
- 1/2 cup sugar
- 1/4 cup flour
- 2 tbsps (1/4 stick) melted sweet butter
- Zest of 2 lemons
- Juice of 3 lemons

Meringue topping:
- 2 large egg whites
- 1/4 cup powdered sugar
- 2 pinches of salt

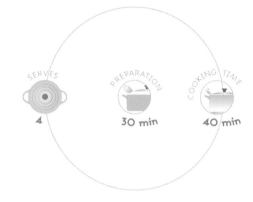

SERVES 4

PREPARATION 30 min

COOKING TIME 40 min

Preheat the oven to 375°F.

Lightly butter 4 mini cocottes.

Gently heat the milk to its boiling point. Take it off the heat and let it cool for several minutes.

Carefully separate the yolks from the whites into two large mixing bowls. Put aside the whites for the moment. Whisk the yolks vigorously with the sugar, flour, melted butter, lemon zest and the lemon juice. Add the cooled milk little by little, without ceasing to stir.

Whisk the egg whites with a pinch of salt, until peaks form, then fold into the lemon-yolk mixture.

Fill each mini cocotte 2/3 full. Place on a baking sheet and bake for 32-35 minutes, uncovered or until the top is a golden brown.

Prepare the meringue topping: whisk the 2 egg whites with a pinch of salt till they form stiff peaks. Add little by little, the powdered sugar. Fill a piping bag 1/2 full and pipe the topping onto each cocotte. Reduce the oven temperature to 350°F and bake for an additional 10-15 minutes or until a lovely golden brown. Serve immediately.

Here is a simpler variation: Skip the meringue topping and just dust the puddings with powdered sugar when they come out of the oven. Easy, and just as delicious!

UPSIDE DOWN PLUM TARTS

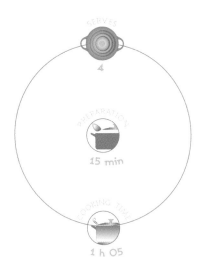

SERVES
4

PREPARATION
15 min

COOKING TIME
1 h 05

- **2 pounds** pitted tiny golden plums (or Red Beauty or Santa Rosa)
- **3 ½ tbsps (scant half stick)** of butter
- **1/4 cup** light brown sugar
- Juice of one lemon
- **1/2 cup** chopped hazelnuts
- **1** frozen pre-rolled pie crust

Preheat the oven to 400°F.

Lightly butter 4 mini cocottes.

Melt the butter in a large frying pan. Sprinkle the sugar over the entire surface and add the pitted plums. Add the lemon juice. Let cook for 35 minutes over a low flame. Add the chopped hazelnuts.

Divide the fruit into the 4 cocottes.

Cut 4 circles of dough slightly larger than a mini cocotte.

Cover each fruit filled cocotte with one circle of pie crust. Press down slightly around the edges, pushing the dough into the top of the dish.

Put all 4 cocottes on a baking sheet covered with aluminium foil.

Bake for 30 minutes.

Let these cool down completely before turning out the plum tarts onto individual dessert plates.

These work well with dark purple damson plums as well. Add the zest and juice of an orange and replace the brown sugar with 1 tbsp of honey.

FROZEN SOUFFLÉS
OF ROSE AND VIOLETTE

SERVES
4

PREPARATION
20 min

FREEZING
7 h

- **8 large** egg yolks
- **1 cup** sugar
- **1/4 cup** water
- **1** vanilla bean
- **2** drops of rose or violette essence

- **2 ½ cups** heavy cream (well chilled)
- **3/4 cup** of liqueur, rose or violette
- **C**olored sugar for decoration

Prepare 4 mini cocottes, lining each cocotte with a 3" diameter by 3" tall tube of parchment paper.

In a large heatproof bowl, whip the egg yolks with the sugar and water.

Place this bowl over a saucepan of hot water (a bain-marie) and whisk without stopping until the mixture thickens (about 4 minutes). Split the vanilla bean in two and scrape the grains into the eggs. Keep mixing this batter until it is thicker and has cooled down. Add the two drops of either flower essence.

In a second mixing bowl, beat the chilled whipping cream until it is thick and forms soft peaks.

Add the liqueur of your choice to the whipped cream and fold into the egg yolk mixture. Spoon each prepared mini cocottes making sure that there are no pockets of air. With a knife, flatten the tops, removing the excess. Put them into the freezer for at least one night before serving.

Peel away the parchment paper, decorate with colored sugar and serve.

These can be prepared up to a week in advance. Make sure that you have room for all of those cocottes in your freezer!

Acknowledgements of the author:

A smiling thanks

to my mother, Romig Streeter, who has inspired my life and my work as a food stylist with her "pots" for the table...and my Poppy, Tal Streeter who has had to put up with two wild cooks in his life!

Loïc Nicoloso who extended the invitation to make this book with him... Also the Le Creuset team who proposed "mini cocottes" and were enthusiastic supporters throughout the whole project.

Hortense Jablonski, our beloved editor at Les Editions Culinaires, Alice Gouget who helped edit the recipes, and Aurore Charoy who did much late night hand holding throughout the english translations as well as shepherding our "mini cocottes" across the Atlantic. Mike Harney and Roger Long, my box friends who both offered sound advice with precision and humor. Karma points to you both, guys!

Acknowledgements of the photographer:

Tender thanks to Severine for her support and constant interest, Yves Bagros for his kindness, confidence and his great energy as well as Hortense Jablonski for commissioning the photographs for this book.

Acknowlegements of the editor:

Thanks to Lissa and Loïc for their talent and efficiency; to Anne for her harmonious layout; to Sophie and Alice for their precious help, and to Johanna of Le Creuset for her professional and enthusiastic participation.

Managing Director
Emmanuel Jirou-Najou

Development and marketing manager
Hélène Picaud

Editorial manager
Hortense Jablonski

Editorial assistant
Alice Gouget

Foreign rights and coeditions
Aurore Charoy

Photography
Loïc Nicoloso

Recipes and food styling
Lissa Streeter

Graphic design
Anne Chaponnay

Layout
Soro and Frantz Rey
for the english version

Photo engraving
Maury Imprimeur

Printed by: The Foundry USA
Legal deposit: spring 2009
ISBN 13: 978-2-84123-256-7

Distributed in the United Kingdom and Export market by
Abrams
72-82 Rosebery Avenue
London EC1R 4RW

Distributed in North America by:
Le Creuset of USA Inc.
360 Concord St Suite 203
Charleston, SC 29401
www.lecreuset.com

And

Stewart Tabory & Chang
An imprint of Harry N. Abrams, Inc.
115 West 18th Street
New York NY 10011
www.stcbooks.com